ke Huron — looking north.

A BOY AT FORT MACKINAC

The Diary of
Harold Dunbar Corbusier
1883-1884, 1892

Edited by
Phil Porter

Introductions and Afterword by
Nancy Corbusier Knox

© 1994
The Corbusier Archives
and
Mackinac State Historic Parks
Mackinac Island, Michigan
3,000 copies

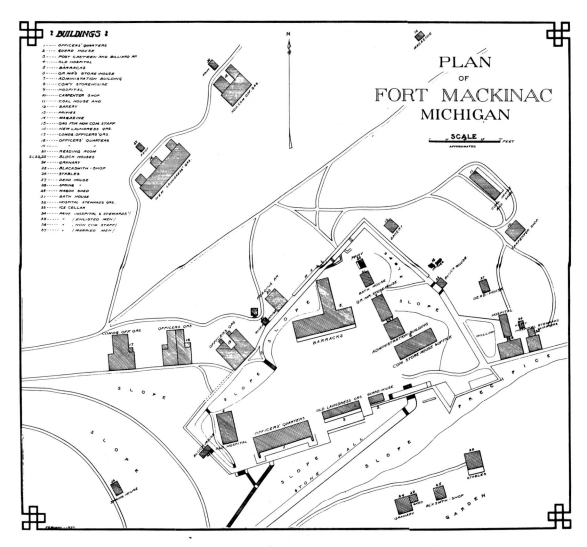

Fort Mackinac in 1890. The Corbusiers lived in house 18. (Photo credit: National Archives)

Contents

Editor's Preface 1

Introduction 1883 5

Diary: January 14, 1883 - September 30, 1884 13

Introduction 1892 79

Diary: June 24, 1892 - August 6, 1892 81

Afterword 97

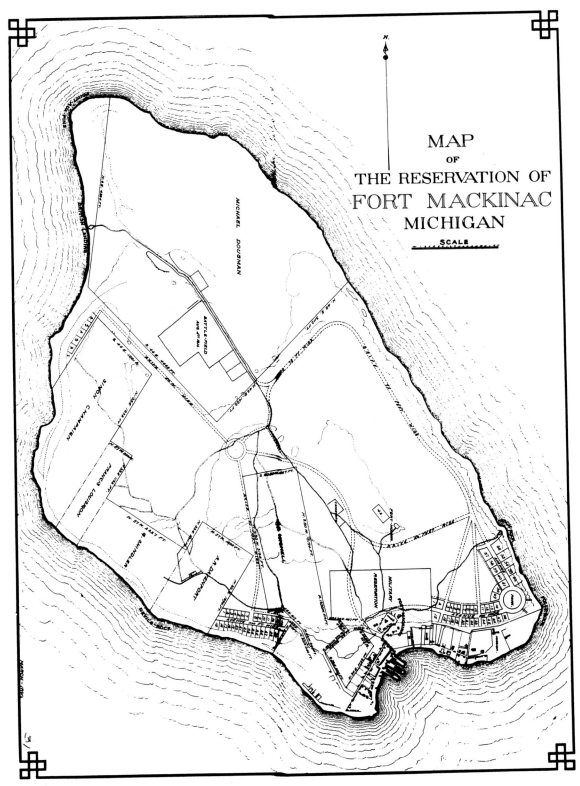

Mackinac Island in 1890. (Photo credit: National Archives)

Editor's Preface

Historians studying military outposts usually focus their attention on the battles, garrison duties, architecture and administrative history associated with the fort. Vast documentary resources provide information on a wide variety of subjects from battle tactics to daily fatigue orders. Often neglected in post histories is the non-military garrison life of a fort; the fort as a community that included a substantial number of civilians, most of whom were the soldiers' family members. Women and children living on military posts were given the unenviable status of "dependents" and their activities are rarely mentioned in official military records. Personal documents, such as journals or diaries kept by soldiers or their wives, are scarce but provide unique and valuable information about the social life of a garrison. Even rarer are the diaries of soldiers' children.

Harold D. Corbusier's diary offers readers a unique and illuminating view of life in a late nineteenth-century miliary outpost. The son of post surgeon Dr. William H. Corbusier, Harold began his chronicle of life at Fort Mackinac as a 10-year old lad in 1883. During his two-year stay at the fort in the 1880s and return during the summer of 1892, Harold witnessed and recorded both the daily occurrences of the post as well as the more substantial social changes impacting Mackinac Island in the late nineteenth century.

The 1880s was a decade of great change for Mackinac Island. Once a prosperous fur trade and fishing village, Mackinac Island became an increasingly popular summer resort after the Civil War. Crowds of tourists and health seekers discovered the island's natural beauty, historic charm and healthy environment and flocked north during the "heated term." The rush of tourists (and the threat they posed to the small island's natural and historic resources) prompted the federal government to establish Mackinac National Park in 1875.

When Harold and his family arrived on Mackinac Island in 1882 they discovered that their island home was a burgeoning summer resort. Visitors from across the Great Lakes journeyed to the island on elegant passenger steamboats including the newly-launched *City of Cleveland* or on board trains which extended their service into Mackinaw City in 1882. Summer travelers found hotel accommodations in remodeled fur warehouses and shopped for "Indian Curiosities" in converted cooper shops and fish shanties. With copies of the island guidebook *Kelton's Annals* in hand, sightseers set off to enjoy the wonders of Mackinac.

Fort Mackinac, once a sleepy one-company post, was now the administrative center of the national park with more than 80 soldiers caring for both post and park. Dr. Corbusier's military responsibilities centered in the post hospital on the east end of the fort. Here he treated ill and injured patients, oversaw the hospital personnel and medical supplies and assisted the commandant in regulating the sanitary conditions of the fort. The Corbusier's family life centered in their quarters on the west end of the fort where Fanny and William raised their active brood of five young boys. It was here, perhaps at the dining room table or lying on the floor in front of the coal-burning stove, that Harold began his diary on his tenth birthday, January 14th, 1883.

Mackinac Island continued to prosper as a summer resort after the Corbusiers left in 1884. Ever increasing numbers of tourists traveled to the island on newer and faster boats and trains. Three of the transportation companies pooled their funds and built the Grand Hotel in 1887 to accommodate their passengers. With the construction of the Grand Hotel, Mackinac Island emerged as the most fashionable resort in the upper Great Lakes, attracting socialites from throughout the Midwest. In keeping with the standard established by "The Grand," prominent industrialists from Detroit and Chicago built magnificent summer mansions on the cedar-lined bluffs overlooking the Straits of Mackinac.

Accompanying the health-seekers and sight-seers were soldiers from Fort Wayne in Detroit who looked forward to their month-long summer encampments on the government pasture west of Fort Mackinac. Harold and his family returned to Mackinac Island when Dr. Corbusier accompanied a detachment of the 19th Infantry from Detroit during a target practice encampment in the summer of 1892. As always he kept his diary close at hand, but now the entries were longer and focused on young ladies and dances rather than the amusements of a ten-year old.

Harold Corbusier left Mackinac Island for the last time on August 6, 1892. One hundred years later, in August of 1992, Harold's grandson Warren O'Brien visited Fort Mackinac, now restored and interpreted to the period of the 1880s. Mr. O'Brien piqued the interest of fort historians when he spoke of Harold's diary and the family's connection with Mackinac Island. Mr. O'Brien's mother, Frances Corbusier O'Brien kindly donated a copy of the Mackinac years of the diary to Mackinac State Historic Parks. Mrs. O'Brien and her sister Barbara Corbusier Pflueger gave permission to share this delightful story with a wider audience through publication.

The diary is presented as Harold left it, complete with the spelling and grammatical errors expected of a ten-year old boy. Additional information about the Corbuiser's stay at Mackinac comes from Harold's mother in *Recollections of Her Life in the Army,* by Fanny Dunbar Corbusier.

Nancy Corbusier Knox, Harold's third daughter, has been instrumental in publishing her father's diary. Mrs. Knox provides valuable family background and personal insights through her introductory remarks and in the afterword. She has also shared several family photographs to help illustrate this delightful story. Mackinac State Historic Parks gratefully acknowledges all of the Corbusier family's contributions in developing this publication.

Phil Porter, Curator of Interpretation
Mackinac State Historic Parks

Fort Mackinac Mich

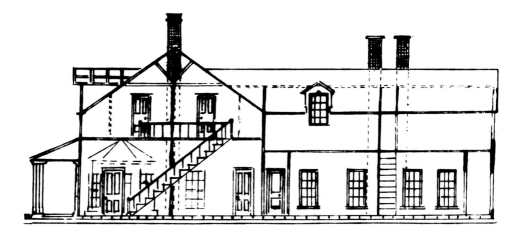

Partial side elevation and cross section.
Company Officers Qrs.

Estimated cost 5505
abb⁴ by Secy War Mar 22/76
See 4987 of 75 – 1197 of 76
Mar 23/76 Order to be sent

Front Elevation.
Company Officers Quarters

The Corbusiers lived in the left side of this double house. (Photo credit: National Archives)

Dr. William Henry Corbusier (Photo credit: National Archives)

Introduction
1883

Queen Victoria had set the style. The 19th century was an era of diarists and keepers of journals. In young Harold Corbusier's case the undertaking was prodded by his father who was precise as a surgeon, demanding as an Army officer. It might have been parental suggestion that the first page of the birthday present be headed, "I am ten years old today." The date was January 14th, 1883, the place Fort Mackinac, Michigan, the penmanship was remarkably mature. Further on the page the birthday lad corrected an oversight, he added, "I was born at Camp Date Creek, Arizona."

Harold Dunbar Corbusier was the second of the five sons of William Henry Corbusier, Medical Department, U.S. Army, and Fanny Dunbar Corbusier. It is Harold's birthday diary augmented by his mother's memoirs that give us an intimate look into the life of an Army child at Fort Mackinac and the quite different view of an adolescent when the family returned to Mackinac eight years later.

William Henry Corbusier was an historian with the conviction that family history must be preserved for the generations ahead, inspired by the celebration of the Centennial of the United States when a country's history was reviewed and a nation's progress was evaluated. He, himself, produced over many years an enormous work of genealogy following the Corbusier family to the smallest twig on the tree and from its ancient roots in France and England to Bermuda from where it made its last jump to America. And he recorded his wife Fanny Dunbar's forebears who arrived on the shore of Maryland from Scotland in the earliest days of Lord Baltimore's appeal for settlers, who prospered in Baltimore and moved on to Louisiana.

The marriage of William and Fanny that took place in her mother's house in a war-saddened Amite, Louisiana in 1869 undoubtedly raised eyebrows in the little town, she a gently reared Southern girl, he a Union Army surgeon stationed there with the 1st U.S. Infantry on what reads as not very onerous duty. Those Yankees were the only ones in the post-war

South who could afford to buy the needlework and the cakes and the box suppers sold at the bazaar that the ladies held to rebuild the Episcopal church. After the years of deprivation and tragedy, when the Dunbars had turned their own house, Dunbarton, to the care of wounded Confederates, it was time again for music and picnics and social gatherings. The families of Amite accepted the young Northerners, William spent his evening with the Dunbars. He and Fanny became engaged, were married and sailed from New York to San Francisco, crossing the Isthmus of Panama on the first of the many thousands of miles they were to travel apart or together in a marriage of forty-nine years, serving at some sixteen Army posts across the country and in the Philippines.

Fanny's debut into the life was abrupt. Fort McDermit, Nevada surrounded by one hundred and fifty uneasy Paiute Indians was in raw, untamed country where much of the time there was not another white woman for a hundred miles. Fanny loved it. Here she learned the tricks of the profession, befriended Chief Winnemucca and the Indian wives, planted a garden, entertained every officer passing through, where even putting together a meal was a challenge, and comforted the women when things went wrong. The gentle Southern girl was a quick study. Here their first son Claude was born.

Harold's birthplace two years later was just as rugged, just as isolated and this time in blazing desert. Camp Date Creek, Skull Valley, Yavapai County, Arizona was accessible by ship down the coast of California, up the Sea of Cortez to the mouth of the Colorado River, there transferring to a paddlewheel steamboat towing a flatboat of none-too-happy recruits up river to Ehrenberg. There a wagon was bought from the Goldwater's store for five days of arduous travel across unpeopled desert to the post in time for Harold's arrival. His first nursemaids were young Apache girls whom his mother watched with some trepidation as they exhibited this new and unusual specimen, a pale blond-haired baby adopted by the tribe and called ''child of our people''. It was an auspicious beginning.

Tracing the Corbusier's army career during Harold's early childhood criss-crosses the country, by buckboard, or by that venerable method of transportation for sick, wounded or Army families, the ambulance, always pronounced, in that case and for some reason, with accent on the first syllable. As the building of the railroads inched across the country there were trips back to civilization to their grandmother in Elmira, New York and a taste of life in a town. A seamstress was called in to outfit them with new clothes, household effects were bought and again the lunch baskets were filled for the next journey, the next post. Fort Macon, North Carolina, 1876. In 1877, Charleston, South Carolina and Chattanooga, Tennessee, and back to the West to Fort Sheridan, Nebraska. Harold, now six, remembered his mother's Fourth of July celebration, the first ever held in the Territory with everyone invited, the Ogalala Sioux from the Pine Ridge Agency, the agent and his men, the men on the cattle ranches, the officers and their families and the soldiers of the Fort. It was the kind of event Fanny Dunbar could never have imagined. Then orders again and packing again for Fort Washakie, Wyoming in 1880.

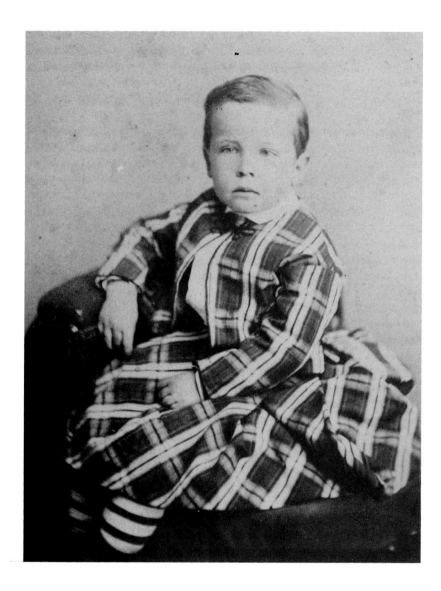

Harold Dunbar Corbusier, age 2 (Photo credit: Corbusier Collection)

The transition from sagebrush, horses and Indians to Fort Mackinac was abrupt as any. When they arrived in April 1883 by boat from Detroit, after again an interlude in Elmira, Fanny wrote, "We had been at stations so much where there were only a few trees, that the woods here were a great delight to us." She describes the setting:

"The Fort stood on a bluff on the south side of the island, and the parade ground, about which the buildings were grouped, was about one hundred and fifty feet above the Straits on a terrace that one could reach by driving up a steep road along the south side of the bluff or one still steeper that led up the west side to the back of the Fort. An old stone building on the south side of the parade used as officers' quarters and two stone block houses with superstructure of hewn logs, built about 1780, still remained of the old Fort. On the crest of the hill a few feet above the parade ground and west of it, were one single and one double set of officers' quarters. We occupied the west side of the double set, which contained three rooms having very high ceilings on the first floor and three rooms with low ceilings above. A gallery ran across the front of the house and from it and our front windows we had an extended view of the Straits of Mackinac to the west into Lake Michigan, and to the east and south into Lake Huron, Round Island, Bois Blanc Island and the southern peninsula of Michigan." She wrote that they burned coal in large base burners and that there was no bathroom or bath tub, nor were there any on the island, and that they had "regular tubbing nights", which pictures an amusing scene of four small boys and a baby being efficiently scrubbed.

Surrounded by an element new to them, there was much to learn; to sail, to fish, to skate and sled and always to explore their island home. Harold and his brothers, each one born at a different Army post (Philip in 1875, Frank in 1877, William in 1882, Army families could call no one place home) were inquisitive, acquisitive, finding treasures in old French and English uniform buttons from the Fort's early history, and, being small boys, were dependably on hand for everything that occurred on the island. They knew the name and arrival and departure of every boat and the comings and departures of every Army family.

By 1884 the officer corps of the United States Army numbered barely two thousand. Fanny Corbusier's memoirs constitute a roster of the personnel of each post where they served, so accurately does she record the transfers and exchanges, the meeting new friends and losing them only to find them again years later, the marriages and the tragedies.

Harold took up the custom and faithfully gives account of the changes in command, but most important at Mackinac, the names, ages, and sex of the eagerly anticipated summer visitors. With them came parties, candy pulls, much music according to his mother, hops (Army talk for dances) at the hotels and speeches, debates and entertainment at the Literary Society. Only once in their first winter does Harold complain that there was "nothing going on in this post", which may have meant that the skating that day was poor, that the snow had melted, possibly there were no boats attempting to break through the frozen Straits, nor was there on that day ice fishing or ice cutting to investigate. The faithful Reverend Stanley never

Fort Mackinac from the island harbor, 1880s.

seemed to fail, if necessary walking across the ice from St. Ignace to give his magic lantern show.

If there was nothing else, he had the weather to report in his diary. For days on end he did, and minutely, the lesson undoubtedly being that accurate observation might lead to accurate deduction. So we must bear with wind, rain, sleet, snow and fog, and varieties of sunny days in all their possible manifestations.

The Corbusiers were no more durable nor remarkable than any other post-Civil War family. The five sons were, however, especially favored in that they were children of parents who placed intense and continuing importance in their son's education. If, as was most often guaranteed, there was no school at a post, they started one. If there were no other children to teach, they taught their own. Sometimes in the West they imported a teacher who at once was put on her or his mettle at the hands of a team of five imaginative boys.

Their mother wrote, "Our boys were far ahead of others of their age among civilians as they were taught zoology, botany, geology, ethnology by Father and knew what was going on in the world." That was no mean feat, we now realize, when mail might take a month to reach their outposts, newspapers were non-existent and most news was learned from travelers or troops moving through. It was not distance but the ice of winter that could isolate them at Fort Mackinac.

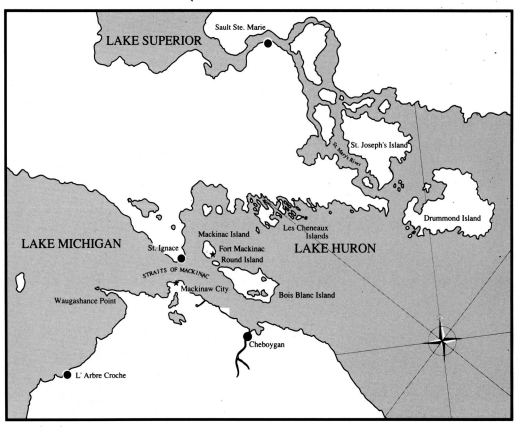

Straits area map.

Harold's lessons in observation extend far beyond the weather. He was acutely aware of sickness on the island and recorded the day to day condition of any afflicted member of the family. "Phil is better today," or "Mama is sick today." Fortunately for them Papa was the doctor. It conjures a picture of a worried ten year old wanting to help, wanting to cheer the invalid, and if this was a foreshadowing of Harold's future it was prophetic, his medical degree from the University of Michigan was a decade or so in the future.

Cousins and friends came to visit, the summer climate was appealing, and the excursions began; picnics, walks, drives to Lover's Leap and Devil's Kitchen and Sugar Loaf. They hired "old Gerome" with his sailboat to St. Ignace or chartered a small steamer to the Cheneaux Islands which, Fanny wrote, "Towed numerous row boats behind for the use of those who wanted to troll for pickerel or pike." She was amused by the women who stayed on board the steamer and caught tubs full of perch. "Some, who had never caught a fish, had to be taught how to bait a hook, caught so many that they tired of the sport."

It was a full and satisfying life. For a small boy there was often unexpected excitement, always it was an expanding experience of learning. But it was also the Army and in September of 1884 came orders to move on, and again back to the West, to Arizona.

10

The Corbusier boys in 1882. (Left to right) Frank, Claude, Harold (age 9) and Philip. Youngest brother William was born in January 1882. (Photo credit: Corbusier Collection)

Fort Mackinac,
Mackinac, Michigan
1883   January   1883
        14th

I am ten years old today
We had turkey and other
good things for dinner. The
ground has been covered
with snow all winter. The
Straits are full of ice except in one place between
here and Round island.
We can see boys skating
near the docks. The Alfgo-
mah has been fast in the
ice near Mackinaw City
since yesterday afternoon.
The chimney in the church
smoked so badly we could
not have Sunday school.
We have been at this post
since April 23rd 1882. O was
born at Camp Date
Creek Arizona

Diary
of
Harold Dunbar Corbusier

Fort Mackinac,
Mackinac, Michigan

1883 January 1883
14th.

I am ten years old today. We had turkey and other good things for dinner. The ground has been covered with snow all winter. The Straits are full of ice except in one place between here and Round island. We can see boys skating near the docks. The Algomah has been fast in the ice near Mackinaw City since yesterday afternoon. The chimney in the church smoked so badly we would not have Sunday school. We have been at this post since April 23rd 1882. I was born at Camp Date Creek Arizona.

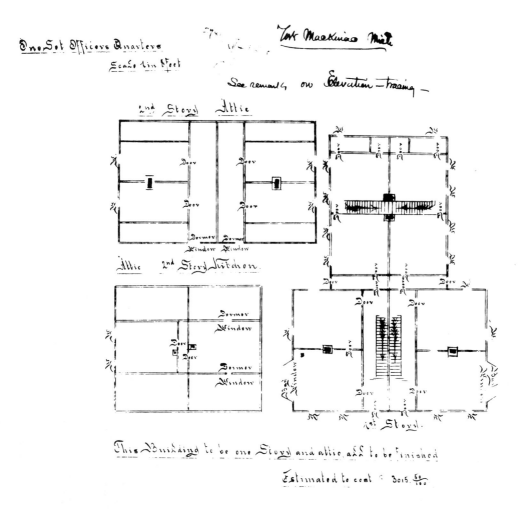

Floor plan of the double house where the Corbusiers lived. (Photo credit: National Archives)

Jan. 15th.

I went to school today. Edwin, Dave and Paulding Sellers, Jeremiah and Ned Ryan,[1] Claude Phil Frank and I Harold D. Corbusier go to the Post School Sergt J. Fred Grant Co. C, 10th Infantry is our teacher[2] We all went skating with Papa today after school. The Algomah went back to Mackinaw City as she could not get over here.

---

[1] *Edwin, Dave and Paulding Sellers were the sons of Post Commander and Mrs. Edwin Sellers. Jeremiah and Ned Ryan were the sons of Private William Ryan and his wife Hospital Matron Joanna Ryan.*

14

Rear view of the west end of Fort Mackinac, c. 1883. Post Commandant Captain Edwin E. Sellers and family lived in the house on the far right. Dr. Corbusier and family lived in the west quarters of the house next door. The post schoolhouse is on the far left.

[2] *"The first teacher was J. Fred Grant, Co. C. 10th Inf., who delighted in telling the boys all the mischievous tricks he did when a boy. They would then do as he had done and once they locked him in the school room to see him crawl out of a window and drop to the ground as his teacher had done. He marched them down to the commanding officer and entered a complaint. The latter dismissed them with a reprimand and the sergeant would march them back to the school again later to tell them about some other mischievous act." Fanny Corbusier's* **Recollections.**

Passenger ferry **Algomah** *in ice off of Mackinac Island.*

16th.

Many men and teams crossed the ice from Mackinaw City to St. Ignace this morning. The skating is very fine. We all went again this afternoon. Mama sat on a sled and Papa pushed her about on the ice. The Algomah tried to come over here to day again and is again fast in the ice.

17th.

We had snow last night and had to sweep off the ice to skate. Rev Mr. Stanley[3] walked over here on the ice from St. Ignace and had church tonight.

18th.

We had fine skating today. Papa had the post snow-plow taken down on the ice, and about twenty town boys dragged it over the ice and cleaned off the snow for us to skate. This has been a bright sunshing day, not at all cold.

---

[3] *Rev. Moses Stanley was rector of Mackinac Island's Trinity Episcopal Church in the early 1880s.*

19th.

Today has been a very blustering day. It snowed all day. The Straits are frozen all the way over to Round Island. The wind piled snow in very large drifts as high as my head.

Jan. 20th.

The ice in the straits has broken up, excepting some around the wharves. We went skating in the afternoon. We all went to Walter Sellers birthday dinner.

Sunday 21st.

Today was a very blustering day and cold. We couldn't go to Sunday School or Church because the chimney smoked.

Trinity Episcopal Church, soon after it was constructed in 1882. The Corbusiers became active members of the new church; Dr. Corbusier ran the Sunday School and organized an adult bible study.

22nd.

It has been very cold today. The thermometer registered 10 degrees below zero, at 7am. The lake is completely frozen over. It was too to go skating today.

23rd.

It is very cold again today, the thermometer registered 10 degrees zero 7am. Two ice boats the first this winter were on the ice today sailing about between here and Round island.

24th.

It is not quite so cold as yesterday but too cold to go skating, The ice is too rough to go skating even if the weather was good. This is a very dull post nothing of interest going on.

25th.

This has been a very pleasont day. We went skating today. It was good skating, the ice is very thick.

26th.

The ice is very thick. We went skating this afternoon. Jerry Ryan walked over to St. Ignace on the ice. He had to walk eight miles to get over there, as the ice was piled up high in places.

27th.

We had snow last night enough to cover the ice so we could not go skating and we could not go over to Round island to see the men spear fish.

Jan. Sunday 28th.

After we had gone up to bed last night one of the chimneys of the Astor-House caught fire and burned for sometime. We went to Sunday School this morning. We did not expect Mr. Stanley today but he came over on the ice this afternoon and held service tonight. Mama and Claude went to church.

29th.

Today the water sleigh was stuck in the snow the men had to take all the barrels out and empty them. It has been quite warm and pleasant.

Soldiers of companies "C" and "D," 10th Regiment of Infantry at inspection in front of the enlistedmen's quarters, c. 1883. Dr. Corbusier is in foreground, second officer from the left.

30th.
It snowed all day. A good deal is melting.

31st.
It has been a very windy and stormy day. The wind is very strong it piled the snow in big drifts. We threw snow balls at Co. C. windows and the men came out and ducked our faces in the snow.

Magic lanterns, which projected enlarged images of pictures painted on glass, were a popular form of entertainment in the late nineteenth century.

1883 February 1883

1st

I weigh 59 ¼ lbs. and am 50 5/8 inches tall. The ice on the other side of the straits has nearly all been blawn away. We boys went down to Truscotts hall to Mr. Stanley show pictures with his magiclaintern.

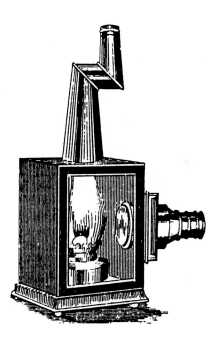

1870's view of the village of Mackinac Island.

2nd.

We went down to the Government dock to see the men cut ice the ice is 17 inches thick. The straits hav all frozen over again. We went to the Mackinac Island Literary Society tonight to here a debate music compositions and speaking.

3rd.

The Algomah has worked her way very nearly over to St. Ignace.

Feb. 4th Sunday.

It is bright but windy, not very cold. We went to Sunday school Mrs. Plummer and Bessie went home today. They went over on the ice to St. Ignace in the mail carriers sleigh.

5th.

The Ther. registered 10 below zero at 7 am. It is clear but very cold today. The Algomah has been to St. Ignace and is nearly back to Mackinaw City tonight.

6th.

It snowed some last night and this morning. It has been cold nearly all day. We went to Mr. Stanleys magic lantern.

7th.

It has been a bright pleasant day. We went skating. It grew cold toward night.

8th.

It was not quite so cold but winday. It snowed little nearly all day. We went skating after school.

9th.

This has been a nice bright day. But cold and winda tword night. We went skating this afternoon.

10th.

It was pleasant all day. We went skating and skated over to Round island.

Sunday 11th.

This has been a very pleasant day. Went to Sunday School.

12th.

It has been a very fine day. Papa went in the one horse sleigh across the ice to St. Ignace, and back.

13th.

This has been the finest day this winter. The Algomah is half way over St. Ignace. Maj Seller went over to St. Ignace in the sleigh.

Feb. 14th.

It has snowed all day, but has not been very cold.

15th.

It has been a cold disagreeable day. The Algomah went from St. Ignace to Mackinaw City I received four valentines yesterday.

16th.

It rained very hard last night. All day it has been very foggy and the snow is melting fast.

17th.

Today has been very cold and winday. Every thing is covered with ice.

18th. Sunday

Today is pleasant till ten oclock then it began to blow and snow.

The **Algomah.**

19th.

This has been a very fine day. We went skating this afternoon. We saw a fisherman setting his nets under the ice. He made three large holes in the ice in a row he tied one end of a string to a pole and passed it down through the first hole, and up through the last one. He cut the string from the pole and tied it to his net. Then a man pulled on the other end of the string and pulled the net into the water. They held it in place by means of sticks tied to each end and laid flat across the holes. To these sticks stones were hung into the water. We went skating. We saw several sleds drawn by dogs bringing home fish nets.

1880s view of the west blockhouse (left) and Trinity Church (right) from the top of Fort Hill. Fort Hill was a favorite sledding course for soldiers and their children.

20th.

Today has been a very pleasant day. It snowed last night and part of this morning. We have been sliding down hill. Maj Sellers went over to the point [St. Ignace] and back, on the ice.

21st.

Today has been winday but sunshiny.

22,nd.

Today has been very pleasant. We all went skating this morning. The Algomah went from St. Ignace to Mackinaw City today. We had holiday as this is Washington's birthday.

23rd.

Today has been windy but clear. We have had a great deal of fun sliding coasting.

24th.

It has been pleasant this morning but windy in the afternoon. We went to St. Ignace today with Maj Sellers we went on the ice.

Sunday 25th.

It snowed all day. We went to Sunday school.

26th.

Today has been windy and cold. The snow has spoiled the skating.

27th.

It has been blowing had and snowing. The Algomah·went from the point to Mackinaw City yesterday and back again today.

28th.

This has been a very pleasant day. We had no school in the forenoon as it was muster.

March 1st.

Today has been very warm and pleasant. Mr. Duggan[4] went to St. Ignace over on the ice today.

2nd.

It has been a bright sunny day.

March 3rd.

It is pleasant again today and the snow is melting. There are not many horses in the village now. Most of the people use dogs instead of horses. They hall water and wood. A dog will hall a very big load. Four dogs are the most I have seen halling.

Sunday 4th.

It has been another pleasant day.

5th.

It has not been so pleasant as yesterday. Mama and Papa went to St. Ignace in the sleigh.

6th.

It has been a very disagreeable day - snowed all day.

7th.

It has been clear but very cold and windy.

8th.

It was quite windy today. We went to a public meeting of the Mackinac Island Literary Society and enjoyed the entertainment very much.

9th.

This has been a very pleasant. A light snow fell about four pm.

10th.

Not a very pleasant day.

---

[4]*Lt. Walter Duggan. 10th Infantry.*

Dogs hauling wood on the ice from Bois Blanc Island to Mackinac Island.

Sunday, 11th.

Today has been very pleasant. We went to Sunday School.

12th.

The weather fine today.

13th.

This has been a very delightful day.

14th.

Today has delightful. It has been thawing a great deal. A large flock of crows has come. A great deal of snow has fallen this winter, It is piled up in places as high as a mans head. People are getting in wood from Boisblanc very fast, as they fear the ice will soon brake up.

March 15th.

It has been very cold today. It is Frank's birthday, he is six years old.

16th.

This has been a very cold day but the sun has shown brightly.

View of Fort Mackinac from Market Street, c. 1880. Captain Sellers' house is on the far left. The Corbusiers lived in the house next door. (Photo credit: Clarke Historical Library, Central Michigan University)

17th.

It has been a very blustering day. All of us boy went to Devils Kitchen twise. we made an fire the first time but the seckond time we could not make one because the wind was to strong. It has snowed by spels today, and rained a little tonight.

18th Sunday.

Not so windy as yesterday but it has been very cold as a north wind has been blowing.

19th.

It has been a bright cold day.

20th.

It has been a delightful day.

21st.

It has been a very pleasant day.

22nd.

An east wind has been blowing today.

View of Devil's Kitchen, c. 1870.

Fort Mackinac with Trinity Church and the government pasture in the foreground, c. 1895.

23rd.

It has been quite warm in the sun today. We all went to Church this morning as it was Good Friday. About three inches of snow fell last night.

24th.

It has been a delightful day.

Easter 25th Sunday.

It has been a mild day. We had Easter eggs. We receved pretty Easter cards in sunday School.

March 26th.

It has been a warm cloudy day. We had holiday as it was Easter monday.

27th.

It has been a delightful and sunshiny day.

28th.

It has been a warm and charming day.

29th.

Today has been as pleasant as yesterday was, and the snow is thawing fast.

30th.

The sun shone all day and has been thawing a great deal. Mama, Mrs. Sellers and Mrss. Dugan went sleigh riding and upset in a snow drift in the park.

31st.

Another bright day. We went to see Mr. Stanley Magic lantern exhibition.

Sunday 1st April.

It has been a beautiful clear day and the snow is melting very fast. We saw the Algomahs smoke south of Bois Blanc. She now makes trips to Cheboygan going north of the Island and east of Bois Blanc. She has not been over to Mackinaw City latly as the ice was to thick.

2nd.

It is a springlike day warmer even than yesterday. But the straits are still frozen over.

3rd.

It has been a delightful day.

4th.

It has been fogy and has been sprinkling all day. The snow is melting very fast.

5th.

It has been a warm day - clear and no wind. It did not freeze all last night.

6th.

It has been a springlilike day. We went to the Literary Club last night. The Algomah past the north side of the Island this morning, on her way to Cheboygan. Men were cutting ice two feet thick on the lake today.

April 7th.

It has been a warm and pleasant day.

Sunday. 8th.

Another pleasant day. Mr. Stanley walked from St Ignace this afternoon. He says there are five and six inches of water on the ice and it is full of air holes. A warm wind is blowing to night.

36

Harvesting ice on Mackinac Island's harbor.

The observation tower at Fort Holmes.

9th.

It has been a windy day but the snow thaued a great deal.

10th.

It has been a raw day. Today is Papa's birthday. He received six
cards and a bouquet. The ice is getting weak in places. We saw
the Algomah today going from St. Ignace to Mackinaw City.

11th.

It has been a cold and disagreeable day. A great deal of the ice
east of the Island has floated away. Dead-Man's hole opened
today.

View from Fort Holmes c. 1895.

12th.
It has been a bright windy day. I predicted a snow storm but it did not come off.

13th.
It has been a bright but cold and damp day. The ice on the south side of the Island is broken up and is floating away. The steam boats are runing from Detroit to Alpina.

14th.
It was raw this morning. After lunch we all went to Fort Holmes.

Sunday. 15th.
The air was fair this morning but the wind blew in the eavning.

April 16.
It hay been a very pleasant day. Yesterday a man was drowned.

April 17.
The last two mails the carrier has brought over in his rowboat and has come round the east side of the Island. It has been a beautiful bright day.

18th.
It has been a cloudy day. An east wind has been blowing. They found the body of the man who was drowned.

19th.
It has been a very pleasant day.

20th.
It has been a springlike day.

*The **Atlantic**, ice bound in the Straits of Mackinac, April 1890.*

Steamer **City of Cleveland,** *launched by the Detroit and Cleveland Steam Navigation Company in 1882, the year the Corbusiers came to Mackinac Island.*

21st.

It has been a beautiful day. The Algomah the first boat since fall came here today at ten thirty a.m. The City of Cleveland came also at four thirty p.m.

Sunday 22nd.

It has been a chilly and cloudy day.

23rd.

It has been a windy but sunshiny day. The Algomah came today.

24th.

This has been a very cold disagreeable day a little snow falling all day.

25th.

It has been a cold and clear day. The City of Cleveland and the Atlantic came in today.

Fort Mackinac's upper gun platform. In the 1880s the fort cannons were used only for ceremonial purposes including salutes to the first vessels of the season.

26th.

When we woke this morning we found the ground covered with snow and it was still snowing by noon the snow had all melted.

27th.

Early this morning there was a dense fog but it cleared away by ten oclock and the rest of the day was clear. The Flora whiseled a long time before she came to the dock as the fog was so thick.

April 28th.

A steam barg past through the straits from lake Michigan they gave her a salute of one gun as she was the first boat of the season. The Sellers boys and we went into the woods at the foot of the hill on the west side of Fort Holmes to gather maple sap. We ate our lunch out here. We taped eleven trees and brought home four galons of sap and would of had more but we wasted a great deal.

Sunday 29th.

The Kweenaw from Detroit tried to get in here but the ice was to thick and she went to St. Ignace. The Lady May a little steam boat which ran between here and St. Ignace last summer and made sevral trips a day came in today.

30th.

We had half holiday as it was muster. The Champlain the first boat from Chicago arrived here after retreat. We went out to the maple trees after sap and brought in a great deal.

May 1st.

It has been a butiful day.

Observation tower at Fort Holmes with rifle range in front.

2nd.

The St. Mary the first boat from the sault came in today.

3rd.

The Toledo from Detroit came in today.

4th.

It has been a very rainy day and is raining very hard tonight.

5th.

It has been a cloudy day the sun has not shown all day.

Sunday 6th.

It has been a warm day.

May 7th.

The weather has been very changeable today it was raining this morning then foggy and cleared off at noon. We heard the frogs singing this evening. We saw 37 sailing vessels in the straits at one time.

8th.

It has been a very pleasant day.

9th.

It has been very disagreeable day.

10th.

It has been a very rainy day and cold.

11th.

It has been a very disagreeable day.

12th.

It has been a very windy and cold day.

13th.

It has been a very pleasant day.

14th.

It has been a very charming day.

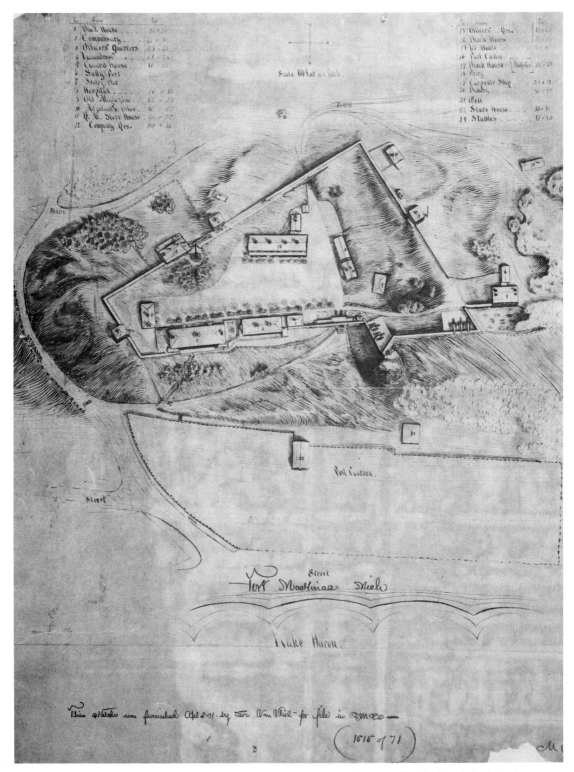

Map of Fort Mackinac in the 1870s. (Photo credit: National Archives)

45

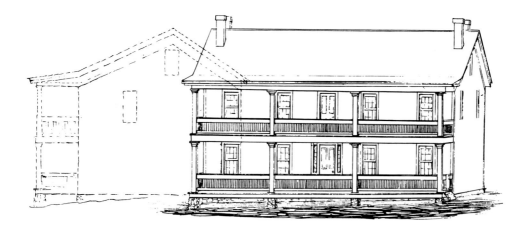

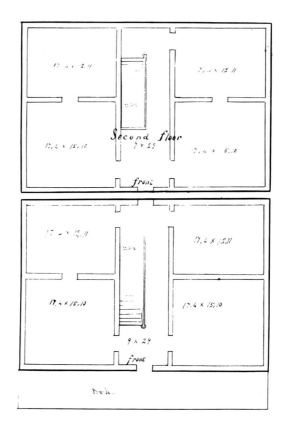

Elevation and plan of the Fort Mackinac Hospital. (Photo credit: National Archives)

15th.

It has been a very pleasant day. It has been Mama's birthday she received seven preasants.

16th.

It has been the best day we have had for a long time. The swallows came today.

Sunday 17th.

It has been a very windy day. We did not go to sunday school today.

18th.

We had a very hard rain today. Papa went to the Point this morning. Phil and Claude went to School this day. Our teachers name is Anderson Crauford.[5]

---

[5]*Private Anderson Crawford replaced J. Fred Grant as post school teacher on May 18, 1884.*

19th.

It has been a very windy.

20th.

It has been a very pleasent ·day.

June 21st.

They begun Artilery drill, for the fourth of July today.

22nd.

It has been a very pleasant day.

23rd.
It has been a very pleasant day.

Sunday, 24th.
We did not go to sunday School today.

25th.
It has been a very disagreeable day.

26th.
It has been a very windy day.

1880's Fourth of July activities in the village included tightrope walk contests between the town docks.

July 4th.

It has been a pleasent day. They fired a sulute of thirty-eight guns at noon we have had a very nice time today down town they had go-as-you-please races, walking maches, pony hurdle, row boat races, greased pole, tub races. Jumping matches. Mama Mrs Sellers, Miss Duggan and Mr. Duggan went to the Point on the Algomah.

5th.

Last night we set off a great many fire works. Claude hurt his hand very badly last night.

11th.

It has been a very disagreeble day Capt. Ward Inspecter on Genl. Hancock staff inspected the post today[6]

---

[6]*Captain Thomas Ward, Acting Assistant Inspector General, inspected the post which was in the Division of the Atlantic commanded by Major General Winfield S. Hancock.*

13th.

Cousin Henrietta and Gertie came today on the Flora from Toledo.

July, sunday 15th.

We went to sunday School this morning and went for a walk on the bloof.

19th.

It has been raining since sunday but is pleasant today. We went rowing this afternoon.

August 3rd.

This is Clauds birthday he is twelve yers oald. We are haveing beautiful weather.

Fort Mackinac's lower gun platform.

Cottages in Hubbard's Annex, Mackinac Island's first summer cottage community established in 1882.

5th.

Bishop Harris[7] preached for us today. This eavening papa and cousin Ettie Gertie went over to St. Ignace to here Bishop Harris preach there. we went over on the Lady May and she was very much croaded. Capt. grummond and a ald steam boat captain stood by the engin room nearly all the way over to see that all was right. Claude and I were on board to.

6th.

We out to the Anex to burn brush for Mr. Hubbard. We took our lunch and spent the day.

---

[7]*Rev. Samuel Harris was Bishop of the Episcopal Diocese of Michigan and a summer cottager in Hubbard's Annex.*

7th.
We went to a panorama of Ireland last night.

9th.
Mama Cousin Ettie and Gertie went to the Sauld Ste. today.

10th.
Mama Cousin Ettie Gertie returned today.

Aug. 13th.
We are having very pleasent weather, and the Hotels are full people. the sity of Macanac made her first trip.

16th.
We have had a festival for the last two days to help the Church

17th
Cousin Ettie and Gertie left on the flora for tolodo.

25th.
The ladies gave a consert last night for the benifite of Rev. Mr. Stanley. Mrs. Dr. Brechemin who is stationed at the Sault Ste Marie to sing.

*The **Flora** moored at the island's town dock.*

Dr. Corbusier (top row, second from right) and his sons Harold (middle row, far right) and Claude (front row, center) pose for a photograph with friends after an August 1884 picnic on Mackinac Island. (Photo credit: Roy Goodale)

29th.

We hired a boat from Davis an rowed around to the other side of the Island past arch rock and had picnic.

29th.

We went in wadeing as it was very warm. We took a big watermelon with us buried it in the sand to keep it kool. Mrs. Sherman from Detroit and her little girl wer wih us.

30th.

I went with Mama and Papa on a excursion around the Island to St. Ignace. we went over on The Algomah.

31st.

Theodore Fletcher who lives out at the Annex took lunch with us today.

Sept 6th.

Phil and I took dinner with Mrs. Sherman at the Mission House. Nearly all the Visators have left the island.

The Mission House in the 1890s. Constructed as part of the island's Presbyterian mission in 1825, the Mission House became one of Mackinac's first summer resort hotels in the 1840s.

September 10th.

We started to school today. Our teacher is named Anderson Crawford. I study Spelling, Reading, Geography, History, Arithmetic, and Writing.

October
Sunday 11th

There was a light fall of snow last night.

16th.

Mr. and Mrs. Fletcher took lunch with us. Blanch took lunch with us yesterday.

22ond

Mrs. Sellers left for Phila. today. Maj. Sellers went part of the way wih her. Mrss Duggan left for Chicago.

23rd.

I have a very bad coald. Papa thinks it is because I had my hair cut on saterday.

24th.

It has been a butiful day. We had our stoves put up today. The Flora has not been this weak Friday.

25th.

Mr. Duggan and Mr. Plummer[8] came from the Sault today they have been there since the 20th. on court Martial duty.

26th.

Papa Claude and I went trowling this eavning. We went over by round Island but we did not catch anything. It has been a fine day.

27th.

We got up early this morning to look at our rabbit traps.

Sunday 28th.

We had church and sunday school this morning.

---

[8]*Lt. Edward H. Plummer, 10th Infantry.*

1880's sentry on duty above the south sally port, with lower gun platform behind.

October 29th.

The weather continues to be very mild. Papa went trowling today he caught two large trout togeather they weighed fifteen pounds.

30th.

It has been a very windy day.

31st.

It has been a very stormy rainy day. It is All Hallowes eve we going to dive for apples but there wre none in town so we had to dive for potatoes we played games and mama made candy I have a headache today.

November. 1st.

It has been a cold but clear day.

5th.

It has been raining hard all day. I had a headache again today.

6th.
It has been a pleasant day.

7th.
We are having very pleasant weather.

8th.
The Dahlia the light house steam vessel raised the bouys today. There was a butiful ring around the moon tonight.

9th.
Papa had to go over to Sheboygan to a man that was very sick.

Sunday 11th.
There was a very severe storm snow sleat and rain fell, the wind blew very hard. The storm lasted all day. We could not go to sunday school.

12th.
There was a light fall of snow last night.

November 13th.
When we woke up this morning the grown was covered, with snow to the depth of six or eight inches. We were sleding down hill all day.

14th.

It is not as coald as yesterday our things come on the City of Mackinac.

15th.

It has been quite pleasant today.

16th

It has been cold but pleasant.

17th.

The snow is thawing very fast today Claude and I made a snow man. We made a snow fort to.

sunday 18th.

The sun has been shining, It has not been cold. We went to sunday school. Mama has a very bad cold.

19th.

The snow is melting fast they say it is not ging to last. Mama is sick in bed.

20th.

It has been a very fine day,

21st.

It rained very hard last night and all of the has gone but a very little bit. The boats are running very irigulary. We hear of a great many shiprecks since the storm of the 11th. On Lake Ontario the wind blew at the rate of two miles a minute.

26th.

last nigh the wind blew very hard and the lightning was as vived as during a summer storm.

November 27th.

We have laid in all our supplies for the winter we can hardly find room enough to every thing. The snow has all melted. It is blowing very hard tonight.

29th.

Today is Thanksgiving day. We boys went skating on the pond. Mama and papa went to church.

December 3rd.

It has been a very pleasant day. The snow is melting very fast.

4th.

We have been sliding down hill in front of our school house. It has been a pleasant day.

10th.

The weather has been quite warm but it turned coald to day. The snow has all melted.

11th.

Willie has disentery. He is quite sick in bed.

12th.

Willie is better to day. We went down to the pond. but it was all slush not fit to skate. Phil and I went down to Mrs. trusket's to learn a song for Christmas. And we went on the 10th for the first time.

13th.

It has been a cold but pleasant day. The weather is very pleasant.

December 14th

It has been very cold to day. Dave [and] Mrs. Sellers arrived from her visit from Philadelphia.

Sunday 16th

It has been a cold day. Willie is a little better.

17th.

There is ice in the straits to day. It blew in from lake Michigan. It is the first time it has been on this year.

19th

They began to dress the Church to day. There is more ice in the straits to day.

20th.

It snowed last night and has been snowing all day very hard. Every body is getting ready for Christmas.

25th.

We had a Christmas tree this mornig. Willie was delited with it, I received the "Theatre Royal." a knife, the Calendar of American History and several other little preasants.

January 1884
Tuesday 1st.

It has been a pleasant day. The lake is freezing over fast. We had Mr. Stanley to dinner today.

2,ond.

It has been a blustering day. The Algomah is stuck in the ice over by Mackinaw City.

3,rd.

The Algomah is still stuck in the ice. Mr. stanly has lent us his dog Oscar because he has to go over to St. Ignace to preach.

4,th.

We went skating on the lake to day for the first time. The Algomah is still stuck in the ice she has been trying to get out but she can not.

5,th.

We went skating to day again the ice is very good we skated all day long.

Sunday 6,th.

We went to sunday school to day.

7,th

We went skating again to day. The ice is splended it is just like glass. We took Willie down to and after we had been dow a while mama came. We had half holiday because the skating was so good

8th.

We went skating to day and There was a little snow on the ice.

9,th.

We went skatining again to day. We had a rid on an ice boat. Papa made a sale so we could sale with it when we were skating⁇

10,th.

It snowed last night and covered the ice. We went skating and sweped a little place to skate on. To day has been pleasant.

⁹*"After the snow rendered the ice rough, father made sails to carry. One kind was on a bamboo pole bent as a bow and carried on one shoulder and another was a square sail to carry on the back, often with a top sail to raise above the head."* Fanny Corbusier's **Recollections.**

Ice boats on the island harbor, c. 1895.

14,th.
To day is my birthday I am eleven years oald. The algomah succeeded in geting over to the Point.

15,th.
The skating is all spoiled from the snow. They began to cut ice to day. It is 11 inchies thick.

Jan.
17,th.
It has been a very blustering day, but not cold. We had a butiful sunset the whole sky a deep rose color.

21,st.
The Algomah has been making regular trips from the Point Mackinaw city she began to make them ever sinc the 18th. It has been a damp windy day.

23,rd.
It has binn a windy day. a little cold. Papa and the boys went skating down by the Mission House they said it was very good.

Hauling firewood in horse-drawn cutters across the ice to Mackinac Island.

29,th.

The people are cutting ice and halling wood on sleds from Bois Blanch and round Island. We went down to see them cut ice with an ice plow. The plow has eight blades one behind the other. A horse is hitched to the plow a man guides him over the ice to cut and another man guides the plow. They cut it in long strips and then men saw it into cakes. Thes bloks they push up a canal in the ice which they have cut and then draw it by means of a grapplin iron onto a platform and then sleighs come and draw it to the ice house to be packed away.

A horse-drawn ice plow scores the ice before the men cut it into blocks on the island harbor.

February 1st.

It has been a very pleasant day. The coasting is very fine. We have been sliding a great deal dow the fort hill it is a hill upon which the fort is built. We start from the top and go down with such speed we go way out on the ice.

2,nd.

We have been having a great deal of fun to day. We were sliding down hill all day. There were a great many on the hill.

Sunday, 3rd

We went to Sunday school today.

4th.

Carry our kook went away to day and left us without any kook.

5th.

We got a new girl to day from the Poin. It snowed last night very hard and it is very deep.

6th.

It has been a pleasant day. The snow is very deep every where.

9th.

This mornin as is was Saturday the boys and papa went to the Algomah. They walked there over the ice. It was a rough walk of ten miles there and back. They saw them sawing her out so as to get her over to St Ignace to be repaired. Iff they leave her where she is when the ice breaks up she will go to pieces. I could not go as I hurt my leg coasting.

Sunday 10,th.

The boys say that they feal tired from there walk.

16,th.

It is quite warm day. We boys have been making snow houses to day.

February
Sunday, 17,th.

It has been a very warm day. We went to sunday school this morning.

*The **Flora** ice bound in the Straits of Mackinac, March 1882.*

18,th.

It has been a warm day just like yesterday. The snow has been melting all day.

22,ond.

As today is Washsington's birthday we have Holiday.

Sunday, 24,th.

We went to church and Sunday school thi morning.

25,th.

It has been thawing a great deal today.

26th.

The snow is three feet deep in the woos, but it is not so high outside.

1884 March !7,th. 1884

St Patric was hung in effigy last night. Today for the first time the crows came.

View of the village from the fort in the 1880s. "Dead Man's Hole" was created by the strong current which weakend the ice between Mackinac and Round Island (in distance).

18,th.

We can see a strip of water way to the eastward. It has been thawing a great deal today.

19,th.

It has been a very pleasant day. The warm weather still continues and the snow is thawing very fast.

20,th.

It has been another pleasant day the snow is melting very fast.

21,st

It has been a butiful warm day. The ice is still strong.

23,rd.

It has been a buttiful day. Dead mans hole is open only in a very little place.

March.
24, th.
Yesterday it was very windy but to day it is calm. It has been a butiful day. Dead mans hole is a great deal larger to day. The snow snow is melting very fast.

25,th.
It has been another pleasant day but the wind blew a little.

26,th.
The Algomah had her wheel fixed and is now on her way to Mackinac City. She is very nearly there. She is forging her way very fast. The water in dead mans whole is very nearly into land. It is very large.

27th
The Algomah failed in her attempted to reach old mackinac [Mackinaw City]. She only went as far as they cut last time when she got there the ice was to thick and she had to turn back to St. Ignace.

28th
The Algomah has made another attempt to go to Old Mackinac. She went back to St. Ignace to get a heavy load as she was to light. They loaded her with heavy logs especialy in the bough.

29,th.
The Algomah has reached Old Mackinaw.

April 6,th.
We were all sick last week Willie is very sick to day.

7,th.
Willie is better to day. Dead mans hole is very large. The Algomah makes regular trips betweene Old Mackinaw and St. Ignace.

April 7,th.
They bring the male over in a dog sleigh because the ice is not strong enough to hold a horse.

Dr. Corbusier cared for ill and injured soldiers in the 1860 Post Hospital shown here with the upper gun platform in the foreground.

8,th.

Phil is very sick![10] Maj. Sellers is very sick also.

9,th.

Maj. E.E. Sellers[11] died last night at ten oclock, of inflamation of the lungs. Phil is still very sick. there has been no school to day on account of Maj. Sellers Death.

---

[10] *"Early in April, 1884, Phil went to the hospital garden to get some horseradish roots that he heard the men were going to dig, and getting his feet wet, wore his shoes all the morning. That night he began to cough and pleurisy developed in his left side. He had to be very carefully nursed, and, to give us a rest, Lt. Duggan often sat with him at night and insisted that I go to bed."* Fanny Corbusier's **Recollections.**

[11] *"During those few days colds were very prevalent, and while the snow was still melting and the air saturated with moisture, Maj. Sellers opened his cellar to look over his remaining winter's supplies, took off his coat while in a perspiration, contracted pneumonia and after only a short illness, died April 8, 1884. He was buried on the 12th and nearly the whole population of the island followed his body to the grave."* Fanny Corbusier's **Recollections.**

12,th.

They had Maj. Sellers funerel today. Almost every person on the Island went to it. Phil is about the same.

Sunday 13,th

We did not go to Sunday school to day. Phil is very sick.

14,th.

Phil was worse this afternoon.

15,th.

Phil is better today. The ice is breaking up very fast. The Algomah in going from St. Ignace to Mackinaw city broke her rudder.

16,th.

Phil is a little better today. We had a wind, snow and rain storm last night. after it froze and the walks have been very slippery. Seldon [Private Walter Selden] one of the Soldigers, died today after a short attact.

April 17,th

Seldon was buried at tow o'clock, Phil is better. The Atlantic came with in about a mile of Robinsons Folly but could not get any further on account of the ice and had to turn back.

Major Edwin Sellers and Private Walter Selden were buried in the post cemetery about one-half mile north of Fort Mackinac.

18th

The Saugatuk from St. Igance came to day about nine, o'clock. The passage is quite clear betwene St. Ignace and here. We have had no mail since saturday. The ice is breaking up very fast Phil is better The Chas. West one of boats and Arnold's tug's came in to day about five o'clock.

19,th

This morning the Chas. West took the lighthouse men to Spectacle Reef lighthouse. The City of Cleavland came up as far as Cheboygan but no further. The Saugatuk broke her boiler so we had no mail to day.

20,th.

Spectacle Reef and Waugashaus light Housees were lighted last night. The Saugatuk brought the mail over from St. Ignace this morning. The City of Cleveland came in at twenty minutes after five this afternoon It is the first boat from Detroit.

21,st.

The Vanralte from the, Salt St. Marie came in this morning for the first time. Almost all of the ice is out of the straits The Light houses are all lighted. The Soldigers began target practice to day.

April, 22,ond.

Phil is better to day. The Saugatuk brought the mail over this morning. Lake Huron is now clear. Lake Michigan still blocked up with ice. The first sail boat was out today.

23,rd.

The Atlantic the the first boat from Toledo came in this morning about half past seven. Phil is a little better to day. It has been a pleasant day.

24th.

It has been a very pleasant day. The flowers are begining to bloom The Vanralte and the Mary came in this morning. The Mary is from Cheboygan. The city of Cleavland came in this afternoon. The Saugatuk brings the mail over every day now untill the Algomah gets a rudder on. Phil is a little better today but is still very sick.

*The **Saugatuck** with the island and fort in background, c. 1880.*

25,th.

The Flora from Toledo came in to day for the first time They gave her a gun from the Fort. They also gave the Saugtuk, City of Cleveland, Vandate, Mary, and Atlantic a gun. It has been a pleasant day. Phil is a little Better.

26th.

The Algomah is fixed She went over to St. Ignace today. Phil is better today. The Vanralte makes trips now betweene here and the Salt St Marie.

April 27,th. Sunday.

It rained today. We did non go to Sundaschool today. Phil is not so well today. We get gum suggar wraped in birch bark.

The wardrobe change from knee breeches to long pants was an important rite of passage for young men in the 1880s.

28,th.
The Sail vessel passed through the straits from Lake Michigan.
Our clothes came today on the City of Cleaveland from Detroit.
We got them at Mables. Claude put on long pants to day for the
first time.

29,th.
The Champlain from Chicago came in to day for the first time.
It has been a pleasant day. and the St Marie came in today for
the first time. She is from the Salt St Marie.

30,th.

The lake has been very rough today. Phil is better. It has been a windy day.

May 7,th. 1884.

It has been a butiful day. Mama has been sick in bed all day. All the ice is gone except a little bit.

2,ond.

It snowed a little this morning but melted soon. Mama is still in bed but she is a little better. Phil is better to.

3,rd.

It has been a pleasant day. Phil is better.

Sunday. 4th

It had been a fogy day. We did not go to sunday School today.

May 5,th.

It was very fogy this morning but cleared off twords evening. The City of Mackinac came in today for the first time. They gave her four guns from the Fort.

6,th.

It has been a very fogy today but it cleared off a little. The Mesenger from Cheboygan came in today for the first time. They gave her also a gun from the fort.

7,th.

The peroutous came in today for the first time. From chicago. She is a large with two smoke stacks. It has been a very pleasant day.

8,th.

The Grand Rapid came in today, but she had been in before. It has been a rainy day.

9,th

It has been a pleasant day. The Sellers family are packing. They are going to Chicago.

Assembly of the 23rd Regiment of Infantry on the parade ground. Companies "E" and "K" of the 23rd Infantry replaced the men of the 10th Infantry in June 1884 and stayed at Fort Mackinac for the next six years.

10,th.

It has been raining a little. Phil is better.

11,th.

It has been a pleasant day.

12,th.

The troops are going to be moved to New Mexico.

13,th.

The Seller's family went away today on the Mary to St. Ignace from St Ignace to Old Mackinaw on the Algomah and there from Chicago on the cars.

May. 14,th.

It has been a very rainy day we miss the Sellers boys very much![2]

---

[12] *"We were very sorry when the Tenth Inf. left, May 13, 1884. Our boys missed their playmates, the Sellers boys, to whom they were much attached." Fanny Corbusier's* **Recollections.**

16,th.

Sergent Marshal[13] the Ordinance Sergant died this morning at four o'clock. He was 84 years old and has not been out of his chair for a year.

17,th.

Sergant Marshal was buried at two o'clock. It has been very pleasant.

Sunday, 18,th.

It has been a little windy. we went to sunday school and Church this morning. A telegram was received last night saying that Co. D. will move in a week or then days.

Sept 3,rd.

Claude left here to go to Lauencevill to School.

1884 September 30,th. 1884

We left Mackinac at seven P.M. on the Ferry boat Algomah. We went as far as Old Mackinaw on her. and then we left Old Mackinaw at Half Past nine. on the cars. Which was in the night time.

Children on the ramp to the Fort Mackinac Hospital.

---

[13]*Ordnance Sergeant William Marshall was stationed at Fort Mackinac longer than any other soldier, having served there from 1848 until his death in 1884.*

The Corbusier family at Fort Grant, Arizona in 1885. 12-year old Harold is on far left. (Photo credit: Corbusier Collection)

The Corbusier family in 1893. (Top row, left to right) Harold (age 19), William and Philip. (Bottom row, left to right) Francis, Fanny, William Henry and Claude. (Photo credit: Corbusier Collection)

Introduction

1892

They had left Fort Mackinac young boys; they returned in 1892 young adolescents. This time the transition from the hot, arid Southwest was gradual. Their four years at Fort Grant, Arizona had been formative years, a young boy's ideal of horses and camping and exploring and the excitement of being on the edge of the so-called Apache wars. But Fort Grant never represented the isolation and hardship of earlier western tours. Their quarters were a substantial house; there was a hall where dances were held; Papa had a carriage; Colonel Anson Mills, the commandant, had a pond built in the middle of the parade. Harold and Constance Mills were photographed standing fully clothed and chest deep. There were visitors and a social life which Fanny eagerly joined.

Short tours at Fort Hays, Kansas and Fort Lewis, Colorado preceded orders back to the east to Fort Wayne, Michigan, and Harold and his brothers' first taste of city life, of city school and the company of many contemporaries. Now in June of 1892 the family joined their father at the temporary encampment at Fort Mackinac of the battalion of the 19th Infantry on target practice, and although Harold wrote that everything looked about the same as it did when they were there eight years before, the point of view is now that of a nineteen year-old. It was as near a summer idyll as could be.

Papa is now called Father; the younger brothers are now "the kids". The daily excitement is still in meeting the boats, and the diary still records the arrival of summer families, but with special emphasis on the names of the daughters. And, quite naturally following, is the importance, as their mother wrote, of the "three hops a week at the Grand Hotel and two at the Astor House, so the children could dance to their heart's content." And dance they did. She adds that although the music at the Grand was excellent the Casino (the dance hall) was badly ventilated which Harold attests with his collar.."as limp as a wash rag when I got back to camp."

Fanny Corbusier noted other changes. "Cottages had been built along the front and sides of the island and the huge hotel, the Grand, just beyond the Government field. There were many carriages in the streets and yachts in the Straits. The so-called 'smart set' was there and the women wore fine gowns." But Fanny preferred the lovely walks and drives in the woods which they had had before.

In July they moved into two large tents and one smaller one which were framed and floored, connected by tent flies and pitched in a field of daisies. Here, she wrote, "We enjoyed ourselves in camp in the open once more. The boys took turns making the fire in our cook stove and put the hominy or oatmeal to cook and, when May (a visiting cousin) and I appeared, helped get the rest of breakfast." It was the kind of life that they all loved, the freedom of the out-of-doors, but still, we read, that the dances at the hotels were "usually attended". And even though Fanny may have been politely amused by the "smart set", she made many lasting friendships with summer visitors.

The troops left the island on July 16th. Harold describes the last moments of encampment when at the last note of the "general" call every tent came down dramatically and precisely together. The Corbusiers stayed on for a few more weeks in their field of daisies, at length having to leave when the island was at the peak of its summer gaiety. Both his mother and Harold wrote, "We were very sorry to go." And that from a nineteen year-old who had had the happiest summer of his adolescent life was quite possibly an understatement.

The government field (today the Grand Hotel golf course) was the scene of numerous summer encampments in the 1880s and 1890s.

Diary

Camp C. A.Wikoff,[14] Mackinac.
June 24th, 1892.

We, Mother, May, Phil Frank Willie & I, started from Detroit on the night of the 20th, on the "City of Alpena". We had a very pleasant trip & arrived here about 7 A.M. on the 22nd. Mother & May have gone up to the fort to stay with Mrs. Maj. Coates.[15] We boys are in the camp. Our tent is very large & holds four bunks, a table that will seat six, two trunks & a set of shelves. Besides these articles of furniture whe have four chairs. Behind our tent, & close to it we have a fly pitched to cook under. The band and headquarters will be up on the 25th. Mrs. Wilder & baby came up with us, they stay in camp but mess at the Astor House. Two companies from Ft. Brady left on the 21st just before the order for them to remain, arrived. Col. Braton the new Col. of the 19th arrived before we left. The men are shooting so as to get through as soon as possible & drill when the Col. comes.

---

[14]*The island camp was named in honor of Lieutenant Colonel Charles Augustus Wikoff, Nineteenth Regiment of Infantry.*

[15]*Major Edwin M. Coates was Fort Mackinac's Post Commander from 1890 to 1894.*

Camp Luce Mackinac Island; Co. C. Kalamazoo Light Guards. (Photo credit: Kalamazoo Public Museum)

25th

The band & headquarters arrived today on the Alpena. Col. Braton & the Adj. Mr. French came.

26th.

Had parade in camp this morning with six companies & the band. The visitors are beginning to come. The Kanes came yesterday, they are staying at the Mission House. Went walking today up to old Fort Holmes. Everything looks about the same as it did when we were here eight years ago.[16] I went with mother & father this evening to call on Dr. & Mrs. Bailey.[17] Mr. Brady[18] has a two months leave. He left today for Leavenworth where his wife is.

---

[16] *"We found that many changes had taken place in the years since we left the island. Cottages had been built along the front and sides of the island and a huge hotel, The Grand, just beyond the government field. There were many carriages and saddle horses in the street and yachts in the straits. The so-called "Smart Set" was there and the women wore fine gowns, but we felt at home in the woods, which were the same although drier and we enjoyed the lovely walks as we did formerly."* Fanny Corbusier's **Recollections**.

[17] *Dr. John R. Bailey was a private physician on Mackinac Island who occasionally served as Fort Mackinac's post surgeon in the absence of a military doctor.*

[18] *Lieutenant Jasper E. Brady, Nineteenth Regiment of Infantry, was stationed at Camp Wikoff from June 1 to June 26, 1892.*

27th.

Today has been the worst day that we have had since we have been here. It has rained all day ever since three this morning. The wind has been blowing a perfect gale. Several tents blew down & we had to prop our ridge-pole up to keep it from breaking. We were all sopping wet this evening. The kids seemed to make more noise & eat more today than they have since we have been here.

June, 1892
28th

Took a long walk in the woods today. We are going to have a hop at the Astor House this evening.

Dr. John R. Bailey with whom the Corbusiers dined.

29th.

Had a fine time at the hop last night. Col. Braton was not there as he was not feeling very well. The band plays at guardmounting up on the hill in the morning and down in camp in the evening. They played at the hop last night. Mother & May have gone to stay with Mrs. Dr. Bailey down in town.

30th.

Went down to the Mission House last night. We had muster in camp & at the fort. Took a walk with the Kane girls out to Arch Rock.

July 1st '92

Went sailing this afternoon in old Gerome's[19] boat. Miss Hamilton gave the party. Several went from the camp. There was quite a heavy sea on so we all got sopping wet but that made it more exciting & we all enjoyed it immensely. The band & Headquarters will leave tomorrow night for Fort Wayne. We will leave as soon as the troops are through shooting which will be about the 10th. I heard from Wayne today and they are all quite lonesome there without the troops.

2d.

The band & Col. Braton left this evening. Quite a crowd came on the Alpena. Mrs. Evans arrived and is staying at the Grand Hotel.

3rd.

I took dinner at Bailey's today. There is some talk of the troops staying till the sixteenth, or thereabouts. The mayor of Mackinac (Preston) was in camp today trying to get the troops to parade tomorrow But Maj. Smith, who is in command, told him that the men may go if they wish but he would not order them out.

---

[19] *"Old Gerome, who spoke a mixture of very broken English and broken French, was a favorite of all, and his sail boat was the one we always hired." Fanny Corbusier's* **Recollections.**

The Grand Hotel.
Built in 1887, the Grand transformed Mackinac Island into the most popular and fashionable summer resort in the upper Great Lakes.

4th. July

They had a few country races & other amussements (?) down in the village today besides these there has been no unusual excitement. The usual salute was fired from the fort & they had a pretty good ball game up there. The Fort Wayne nine played the Fort Mackinac. The score was 3 to 1 in favor of Fort Wayne. There was a hop at the Grand Hotel this evening. I danced twelve dances. I am beginning to waltz a little.

Grand Hotel ballroom.

The Early Farm on the north side of the island, c. 1900. (Photo credit: Library of Congress)

5th.

We went on a picnic today with mother & Mrs. Bailey. We got a three seated rig & drove out to the North side of the Island. We found a cave which we expect to explore tomorrow. We are all quite tired after our tramp. Went to a hop at the Astor House this evening danced about eleven dances.

6th.

Quite stiff this morning but we all started about eleven o'clock to explore the cave that we found yesterday. Two of the soldiers went with us. I went down into the hole, with a rope fastened around me, for about 20 ft. then the rest came down & we went a little farther following a large crack which crossed the cave. We all came out covered with wet clay from head to foot. After we had taken a swim in the lake we returned by way of Early's farm. There was a hop at the Grand tonight but I did not go but went to the Mission House where a number of young people assembled to spend the evening. We came home about eleven after playing the banjo and singing (?) most of the evening. Miss Rome Wendell was there. I used to know her when she was a little girl. Her sister is now Mrs. McKinnen.

[The following is an insert from a newspaper.]

Dr. Corbusier and sons made a partial exploration of the new-found cave, mentioned in this column some time ago. After penetrating about 60 feet they came to a quite large chamber with branches leading away in different directions, which they did not explore at the time but will hereafter make thorough examination of. The cave is in the west center of the Island and we expect wonderful developments. Right here we christen the new cave—"The Corbusier." As the exploration progresses we will tell you of it.

The Massey. House

Mrs. W. H. Corbusier, wife of Captain Corbusier of the medical corps of the army, with her sons, are living in tents on the Fort field, a pleasant way for an outing.

7th.

Took May & Miss Wendell for a short row then took mother & father out for a little while. Father is ordered to the State troop's encampment this August to inspect their Medical Corps. We heard last night that the troops will not go home till the 16th prox.

Fort Mackinac with post gardens (now Marquette Park) in foreground, c. 1890.

87

The John Jacob Astor House on Market Street. Formerly the western headquarters of the American Fur Company, the buildings were remodeled into a resort hotel in the 1860s.

8th.

Went to call on the Hamiltons & Brookses[20] this evening then went & danced a few dances at the Astor House but as I didn't like the crowd I left very soon. We are having delightfull weather. It is quite warm during the day but always cool at night. The "Idler" a sailing yacht from Chicago arrived today. She is owned by Cudahy, a pork man that city.

---

[20]*The Hamiltons owned a cottage on the island's East Bluff and the Brooks summered at Mission Point.*

9th Saturday.

Capt. Baldwin of Gen. Miles's staff is here as inspector of small-arms-practice. He is very much put out that the two companies from Brady left so soon and says that he cannot see why these troops are trying to get through so soon as they were ordered to remain for two months. Went to the hop at the Grand this evening and had a very pleasant time. Their hall is quite small and gets very warm especially when there is a crowd as there was this evening. The Grand is filling quite rapidly, every boat brings a number of passengers. The Halls have left Wayne. Capt. Hall is ordered to Maine to inspect State troops.

I think Claude and the Sterns boys will be here about Thursday. Father wants me to go to the Schneauxs with them but I would rather return with the troops.

The troops are going to march to Chicago to the "Worlds Fair" in October.

I went out the other day & tried to sketch one of the old blockhouses. Had a horse-back ride a few days ago. It was the first time I had been on a horse for two years & it felt very good although it was pouring down rain.

West Blockhouse, Fort Mackinac, c. 1895.

10th. Sunday

It has been quite warm today. We heard that Claude would not be here till next week. He starts Saturday which will bring him here on Monday. Went down to Brooks's with father this evening.

11th.

Old Mr. Sheely from Detroit came in on the City of Mackinac this morning. We saw in a St. Ignace paper an account of the cave we explored a few days ago & that it has been named Corbusier Cave. It rained this morning but cleared off in the afternoon. There will be a hop at the Grand this evening. The Revenue Cutter Tiessendon anchored in the bay this morning. The troops will leave next Saturday but our family will remain in camp, in one corner of the field, for a while longer.

Soldiers rest from their encampment duties to have their picture taken, c. 1892.

View of an encampment on the government field from Fort Mackinac,
c. 1892.

12th.

Went to the hop last night but only danced four or five dances.[21]
It was very warm, my collar was as limp as a wash-rag when I
got to camp. There are a number of people at the Grand now.
Most of them come up to show off their silks & sit around where
they can be seen by everyone.

16th.

The "General" sounded today at one o'clock and as the last
note died away all the tents came down together and the men
gave a long yell. They marched to the dock about 5:30 and the
boat started at 11:30 P.M. This evening there was a magnificent
aurora. Flashes of all colors darted out from a circle overhead
and it was so light that a person could read, for a few minutes.

---

[21]*"There were three hops a week at the Grand Hotel and two at the*
Astor House so the children could dance to their heart's content. The music
at the Grand was excellent, but the Casino was badly ventilated and there
were only narrow boards against the walls to sit upon. At the Astor the
room was a fine one, but the music was not so good." Fanny Corbusier's
Recollections.

Grand Hotel with government pasture in foreground, c. 1890.

17th. Sunday.

Mother & May came into camp last night. We are very nicely situated in one corner of the Government field. We have one large Hospital tent which is our parlor and mother's & May's bedroom. Besides this we have three wall tents also two flys pitched behind mothers tent. We use one fly to dine under and the other for a kitchen where we have a range put up so the pipe just comes outside the edge thus protecting all the stove except the boiler. Phil & Frank occupy one tent & Willie & I the other. They are arranged in a square facing a court.

18th.

The boys, Claude, Messers Albion & Waland Sterns; & Rankin arrived this morning from Detroit on the City of Mackinac. We brought them up to camp & gave them a good breadfast. They will stay with us untill tomorrow morning when they will go to the LesChneaux Islands & camp. Each one has a canoe & they intend to do a great deal of fishing. Everyone has a tremendous apetite. This morning all of us boys went for a long walk. It began raining this afternoon and has not let up yet. There is a

View of the fort from the field, c. 1892.

hop going on at the Grand. Claude & Phil have gone but the rest of us are in camp amusing ourselves in various ways.

19th.

The boys left for the Les Cheneaux Islands this morning. They each have a canoe & intend to find a lonely island & camp there.

20th.

Met a crowd down town today and went for a short walk then hung around the beach. One of the girls dropped a bracelet into the lake and after hunting for about an hour we fished it out.

21st.

Went for a walk today with May, Theo Casey, G. Kane and some others. The Alpena came in today. Lizzie Fletcher & Miss Withmin from Detroit came on her. One of the excitements of the day is going down to meet the boats. The Detroit boats come in four times a week. A party went to the Cheneaux yesterday & said they saw the boys camp. We have not heard from them yet or seen any of the immense fish they promised to send.

27th.

The boys came in today. They have not seen a razor for two weeks and of course have a fine growth of whiskers. They are also very much sunburned and looked very tough all over. Geo. Elliot came up on the Flora this morning & is going back with them.

30th.

Camp has been very lively all day except when most of the crowd were out in the woods. Claude & I went out to see the Fletchers this afternoon.

31st. Sunday

The campers left on the Alpena last night and they were very sorry to go but had to get back to work. We hear that the troops from Wayne are going to march to the Militia incampment. They had not expected to go. Went to the Grand hop last night. Mackinac is now very gay and there was a perfect jam at the "Cacino". All the rooms at the Grand are ingaged and there are about sixty cots in the parlors.

1st August

Went out to the creek today with the Brooks two young ladies who are visiting them. Stewart White & Theo. Casey were also in the party making eight in all. We rode out in a two seated rig & had a very gay time.

August 6th.

We left Mackinac this evening on the City of Alpina. We are all sorry to leave but have stayed now, longer than we intended to at first.

Passenger steamer **City of Alpena.**

Harold Corbusier in 1896 while attending the University of Michigan.
(Photo credit: Corbusier Collection)

A Fong   HONG-KONG.

Lt. Harold Corbusier, Acting Assistant Surgeon, U.S. Army, during the
China Relief Expedition in 1900. (Photo credit: Corbusier Collection)

Afterword

Harold Dunbar Corbusier was born on January 14, 1873 at Camp Date Creek, Yavapai County, Arizona Territory, the second of the five sons of William Henry Corbusier, U.S. Army Medical Corps and Fanny Dunbar Corbusier. His early education was received from his parents who were often stationed at isolated Army posts throughout the West. He graduated in 1899 with the Degree of Medicine from the University of Michigan and in 1900 became Acting Assistant Surgeon, U.S. Army on active duty in China and the Philippines. He served as surgeon with the New Jersey National Guard on the Mexican border in 1916 and during the First World War organized the orthopaedic division of the U.S. Army Medical Corps and formed a Base Hospital for overseas duty. He did the pioneer work in recruit rehabilitation and "manpower salvage" in wartime. He became Colonel in the Medical Reserves in 1926.

Dr. Corbusier married Louise Shepard, daughter of Mr. and Mrs. Freedom G. Shepard of Battle Creek, Michigan, who had been a classmate at the University. They had three daughters. In private practice Dr. Corbusier was consultant in orthopaedics to several hospitals and conducted a private orthopaedic clinic in Plainfield, New Jersey.

At his retirement Dr. and Mrs. Corbusier built a house, Sol y Sombra, in Santa Fe, New Mexico in sight of the ruts of the old Santa Fe Trail which he had traveled as an infant with his parents in 1885. Dr. Corbusier died in Santa Fe in 1950.

Harold and Louise Corbusier with daughters (left to right) Frances, Barbara and Nancy in 1916. (Photo credit: Corbusier Collection)

View of Fort Mackinac